ZHANG HENG

AND THE INCREDIBLE EARTHQUAKE DETECTOR

BY RANDEL McGEE

FAMILIUS

Library of Congress Control Number: 2021938983
ISBN 978-1-64170-168-6
eISBN 978-1-64170-385-7
KF 978-1-64170-409-0
FE 978-1-64170-433-5

Printed in China

Edited by Lacey Kupfer Wulf
Illustrations by Randel McGee
Book design by Derek George
Cover design by David Miles, Carlos Guerrero, and Derek George
10 9 8 7 6 5 4 3 2 1
First Edition

I want to thank Zoot Velasco for commissioning me to do a storytelling
performance based on earthquakes. This was one of my favorite stories,
and though I did not use it in my presentation, I was able to turn it
into this book. Thanks also to Christopher Robbins and all the Familius
family for their help and guidance. Forever thanks to Marsha, my wife,
for her help with this book and everything else!

This story is based on a real person and his wonderful invention. The author has taken the liberty to add an inspiring dream to the story for dramatic effect.

China has a long history of shadow puppet theatre to tell the tales of heroes, both real and imaginary. The author is a shadow puppeteer and chose to share this story in the style of a traditional Chinese shadow puppet play.

Z hang Heng was a clever man, perhaps the cleverest in all China. His sharp eyes always noticed the little details in the world around him and the skies above. His talented hands were always tinkering, improving an old machine, or inventing a new gadget. When he made something especially clever and helpful, he said to himself, "Ah, this feels right!"

Zhang Heng attracted the attention of the emperor of China. He was appointed to be the imperial astrologer, but over time the emperor appreciated Zhang, not only for his excellent service, but also for the many clever things he made and did. The emperor praised and rewarded him often.

The emperor's courtiers envied the praise and rewards he received.

They wanted him removed
from the palace. They watched
him for any signs of mistakes.

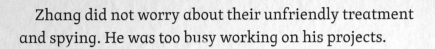

Zhang did not worry about their unfriendly treatment
and spying. He was too busy working on his projects.

China has always had frequent earthquakes.

Legends claimed that great dragons had power over the air, rivers, and seas of China and were the cause of earthquakes. Whatever caused them, the earthquakes left terrible destruction behind in towns and villages.

The young new emperor Shundi was concerned about the earthquakes. A little trembling in the imperial capital usually meant that a bigger earthquake had struck somewhere and there were damages and injured people. The emperor did not know where the earthquake had hit until days later and by that time many lives were lost and property damaged beyond repair. Shundi cared about his people. What could he do?

Emperor Shundi asked his courtiers, "How can we tell where an earthquake strikes?" The courtiers discussed among themselves, but none could think of a way to determine where an earthquake had happened. However, they did come up with an idea to get rid of Zhang Heng.

"Your highness," said the most jealous courtier. "*If* Zhang Heng is as clever as he seems, why don't you *require* him to solve this earthquake problem? If he cannot, then perhaps he is not worthy to be here."

The emperor called Zhang Heng to his throne.

"You are by far my cleverest advisor!" declared the emperor.

Zhang smiled modestly. The courtiers rolled their eyes and frowned.

The emperor said, "Earthquakes cause so much destruction among our countrymen. So many could be saved, towns and villages rebuilt faster, if only we knew where and when an earthquake strikes."

"So, Zhang Heng, I now give you this task to detect earthquakes," declared the emperor.

Zhang was surprised! "How am I to do this, your majesty?"

The emperor shrugged and said, "You are the clever one in these things! You will find a way!"

The courtiers smiled wickedly among themselves.

Zhang began to work right away. He studied all types of devices that measure movement. For days and nights, he drew sketches of devices. Most of them he threw away!

He made models of machines. His assistants stomped on the floor to see
if the machines showed where shaking had come from, but nothing worked.
He did not give up. "Something will feel right!" he said.

One night, Zhang had a dream. He saw eight dragons flying through the sky. Each dragon carried a huge, round pearl in its mouth. The dragons flew in from the eight directions of the compass. The dragons landed on a great egg, each one facing the direction it had come from.

Eight giant, wide-mouthed toads hopped up to the egg and stopped under each of the eight dragons. The toads looked up and opened their wide mouths in a funny smile. It looked like the toads wanted to play catch with the dragons and their pearls.

When one of the toads wiggled its body, the ground underneath it shook, and the dragon above it dropped the pearl into the toad's mouth.

Zhang thought as he dreamed, "The dragons will only feed the toads that shake the ground! The dragons will show me where the earthquake is!" Then he awoke. As strange as it was, the dream felt right!

Excitedly, Zhang sketched a design of an egg with eight dragons and toad-shaped pots under the dragons.

Inside the egg, he devised rods and levers that could move the dragons' jaws and drop the balls into the toads' mouths.

It was by far the cleverest creation he had ever made! When it was done, he said, "Ah, this feels right!"

Everyone in the palace was impressed by the artistry and craftsmanship of the device. The eight dragons looked lifelike. The toads on the ground beneath the dragons looked so funny that many laughed aloud.

"It looks amazing! But does it work?" asked the emperor.
"I am confident it will, your highness!" said Zhang Heng.
"We shall see!" huffed the jealous courtiers.

Days passed, and nothing happened. The courtiers made jokes about Zhang's dragons and toads. With each passing week, they mocked that the dragons did nothing but collect dust. He smiled and said, "I am sure it will work."

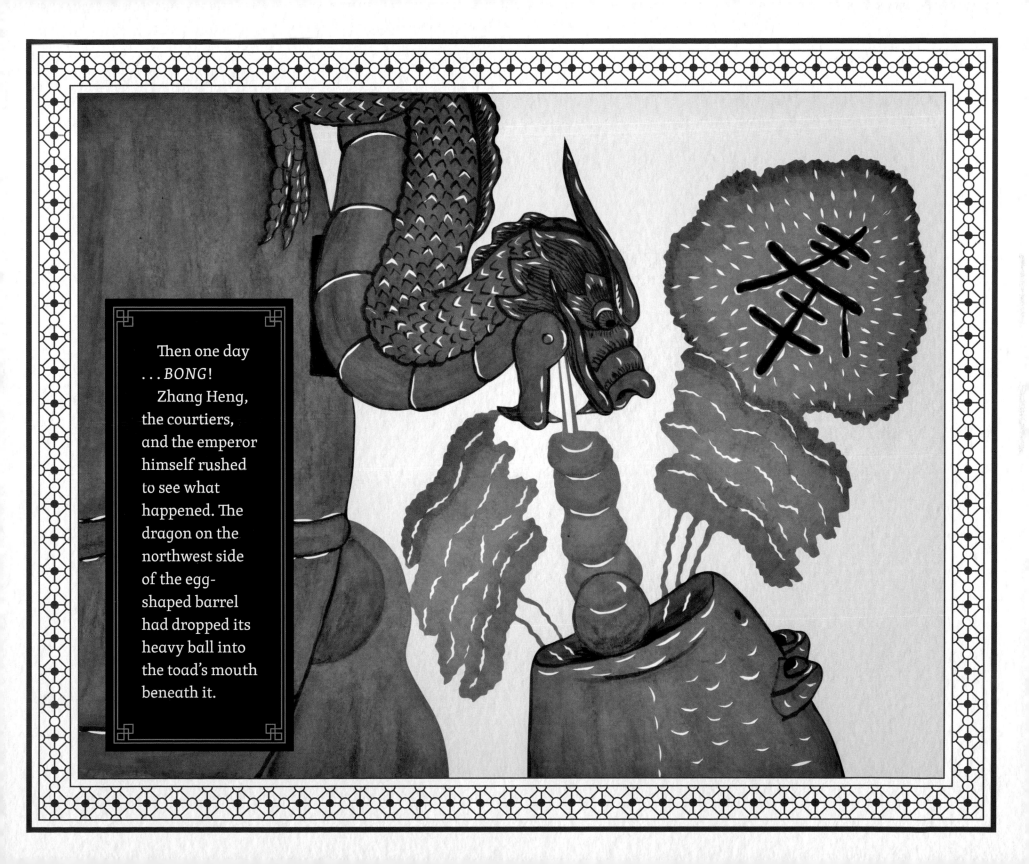

Then one day
...*BONG*!
Zhang Heng, the courtiers, and the emperor himself rushed to see what happened. The dragon on the northwest side of the egg-shaped barrel had dropped its heavy ball into the toad's mouth beneath it.

Zhang Heng exclaimed, "It works! There must have been an earthquake to the northwest! Let's send help that way as quickly as we can!"

A courtier said, "I did not feel an earthquake, your majesty."

"Neither did I," another courtier exclaimed. Soon the emperor himself said, "I did not feel an earthquake either."

"Obviously this device is not working," said a courtier. Perhaps we have placed too much hope in Zhang Heng's abilities."

"It may be so!" said the emperor rather sadly.

Zhang reviewed his designs and the device, trying to figure out if something had gone wrong. He felt that it must have worked correctly. Why didn't they believe the earthquake dragons?

People avoided him and talked in whispers as he passed by. The jealous ones made rude jokes about his dragon toy and the toad pots. After the second day, Zhang sadly started to pack his things to leave the palace.

Three days after the northwest dragon had dropped its ball, a ragged messenger was shown before the emperor, where he declared, "Oh, mighty Emperor, I have ridden day and night to tell you that the city of Longxi in the northwest has been destroyed by an earthquake, and your people there plead for aid as soon as possible!"

The emperor and the courtiers all looked at Zhang Heng.

"It seems I owe you an apology," said the emperor. "Your earthquake dragons did tell me where and when an earthquake struck! Now we must go even faster to aid our people in Longxi."

As the emperor's soldiers and builders gathered together supplies and wagons, the jealous courtiers scowled.

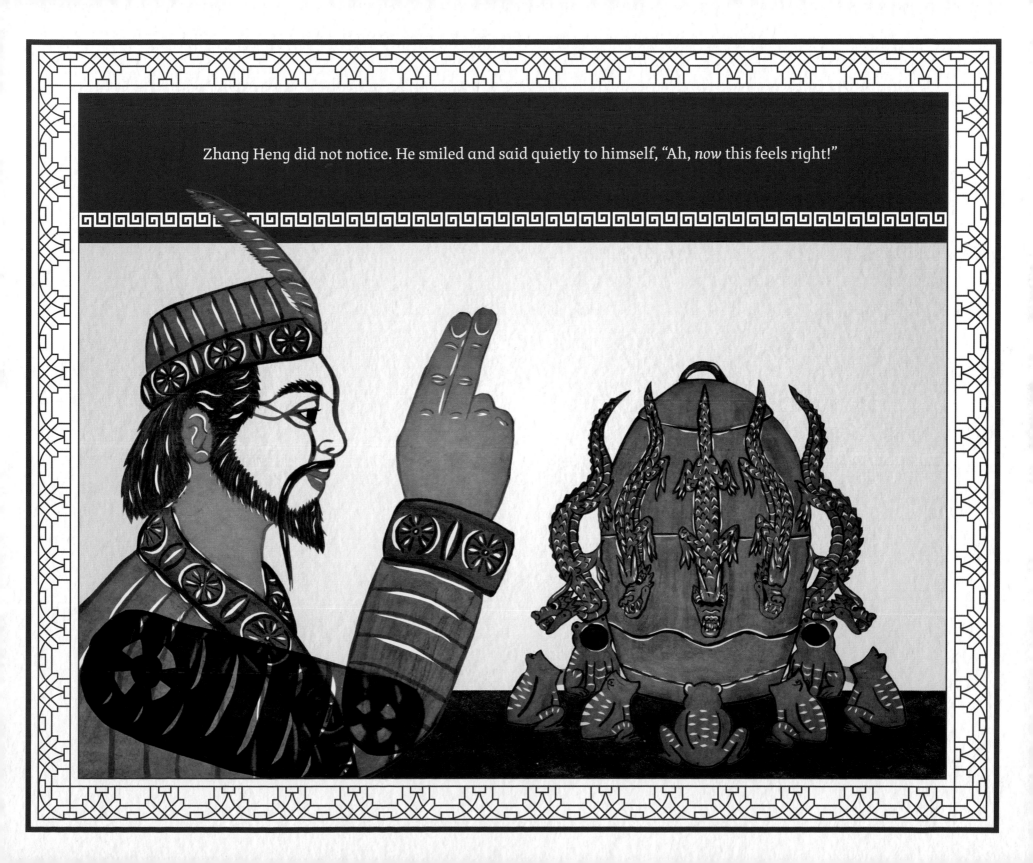

Zhang Heng did not notice. He smiled and said quietly to himself, "Ah, *now* this feels right!"

HISTORICAL NOTES

Emperor Shundi of the Han Dynasty became emperor of China at age ten. He was a kind young man but did not always choose the best councilors to help him rule his people. He died at the age of thirty.

The first seismoscope was made in China in 132 CE by Zhang Heng. He called it *houfeng didongyi* (instrument for measuring the seasonal winds and the movements of the earth). No one knows what inspired him to create his marvelous machine with that specific design. Perhaps it was a dream.

Though the original inner workings of this seismoscope were lost with time, scientists in 2005 successfully recreated a similar device that could show when and where an earthquake hit.

Today Zhang Heng is still honored and considered one of China's greatest scientists for the many advancements he made in astronomy and mathematics. He died at age sixty-one.

GLOSSARY

Astrologer: a person who studies the stars and planets to plan calendars and events

Councilor: a member of a group of people who give advice and council

Courtier: A person who serves in a royal court to help an emperor, king, or queen

Emperor: A ruler of great power over a large area or empire

Imperial: Relating to an emperor or an empire

Seismoscope: A device that indicates the occurrence of an earthquake